SETTING

THE

STAGE

DEDICATION

This book is dedicated to women who were not given proper guidance or knowledge in how to grow into a virtuous women, fearless mothers, or dedicated wives in accordance to biblical scripture. It is my hope that women all over the world would greatly benefit from this and become better prepared for life the right way. I take pleasure in helping others, so for me to have this platform is truly a blessing.

A special dedication to my mother, Denise A. Daniels– devoted, faithful, and loving woman of God. You are always in my fondest memories and will eternally have a piece of my heart.

Table of Contents

INTRODUCTION

This is book is designed to equip women with the fundamental skills and knowledge it takes to be successful in the many roles God has given us.

I desire that every reader of this book will be blessed, empowered, and have a clearer understanding about themselves.

BECOMING A WOMAN

CHAPTER ONE

CREATION

In this chapter, we will explore the process of our creation and how it relates to our daily lives. Many of you will learn from the scriptures— the foundation God established from the beginning— for us to be helpers to our husbands.

After understanding the significance of the creation process, it is my goal that your self-value will increase based on the word of God alone.

Now, let's start with reading scriptures related to God's creation of us. These verses should enable you to value being a woman in today's world.

It is my goal that your view will be forever changed in a positive way.

Genesis 1:27 says:

"So, God created man in His own image, in the image of God created He him: male and female created He them."

Genesis 2:18 says:

"And the Lord God said, it is not good that man should be alone; I will make him a help meet for him."

Genesis 2:21-23 says:

"And the Lord God caused a deep sleep to fall upon Adam, and he slept: and He took one of his ribs, and closed up the flesh instead thereof; And the rib, which the Lord God had taken from man, made the woman, and brought her unto the man. And Adam said, this is now bone of my bones, and flesh of my flesh: she shall be called Woman, because she was taken out of Man."

God shows us the importance and value of our role as women. He creates us from the man which places an inner desire for us to help. After joining the two God gave them a commission to be fruitful and multiply. In doing so they would have children who would continue the process of multiplying upon the land. God is awesome to give us the ability to procreate and keep our legacies going. Now we will discuss the differences between men and women.

As women it's in our nature to want to help men, most times it doesn't matter if he is good for us or not. Our innate ability to nurture, help, and multiply is a superpower given from God. Just as God built us with specific attributes, he also gave the men attributes as well. In contrast men naturally are physically active because of God's command for them to work tilling the ground meaning labor.

So, if a man isn't providing for his family most times, he will begin to feel inadequate. Another aspect to review is how men and women communicate. Men tend to need affirmation, respect, and nurturing to feel loved.

On the other hand women feel loved with physical touch, compliments and attention. In closing just because we're different doesn't mean God can't bring a couple together for his glory and purpose.

QUESTIONS & ANSWERS

What role did God create the woman to fill?

_____

_____

_____

_____

_____

_____

In the Garden of Eden after God blessed them, what did He tell them to do?

_____

_____

_____

_____

_____

_____

God established what institution in the Garden of Eden?

_____

_____

_____

_____

_____

_____

Name something that only women can do.

_____

_____

_____

_____

_____

_____

Can we learn something from Eve?

_____

_____

_____

_____

_____

_____

_____

CHAPTER TWO

AFTER THE FALL

In this chapter, we will review the story that most believe changed the history of the world. The fall of man in the Garden of Eden. As we read in the Bible, God instituted new instructions for man and woman after their disobedience to Him. Here's a quick look at how it all started.

<u>Genesis 3:6 says</u>:

"And when the woman saw that the tree was good for food, and that it was pleasant to the eyes, and a tree to be desired to make one wise, she took of the fruit thereof, and did eat, and gave also unto her husband with her; and he did eat."

We see in the above verse that Eve's downfall started with her eyes (it looked good), she then went all the way with her disobedience. When God approached, them He questioned Adam because he was the leader of the two. Adam responds by blaming it on Eve.

Many of you may have an idea from hearing childhood stories about Eve eating an apple from a forbidden tree. The truth is that the Bible never specifies what that fruit was. So, we will look at a few verses to understand better how all this relates to our lives today.

As we begin with God asking Adam— who was the head of Eve— to explain to Him what happened in the garden, you will see he redirected the blame on Eve. So, it begins to be a blame game to avoid getting into trouble.

Now let's read the following verses to see how it unfolds:

Genesis 3:12 says:

"And the man said, the woman whom Thou gavest to be with me, she gave me of the tree, and I did eat."

Then God questioned Eve, who blamed the serpent.

Genesis 3:13 says:

"And the Lord God said unto the woman, what is this thou hast done? And the woman said, the serpent beguiled me, and I did eat."

We all know that disobedience brings about consequences. We will see in the scriptures the consequences brought on the woman, Eve, due to her disobedience to God. They are as follows:

- Intense pain during labor & delivery
- Craving/Longing (desire) for thy husband
- The husband shall rule (dominion) over the wife

It is best to live according to God's plan for our lives because when we do, it benefits us. We must be careful *not* to just focus on what we see. Our eyes can get us into a lot of trouble spiritually, if we're not able to have self-control.

In recent years the roles of husband and wife has evolved. Now we have stay at home dad's who support their wives going out in the workplace. In Biblical times the women generally stayed at home to teach the children while handling household duties. Now that doesn't mean that women didn't do anything constructive, as a matter of fact the Proverbs 31 woman would be considered an entrepreneur.

Let's look at her a little closer

- scripture says "she works willingly with her hands"
- scripture says "she makes food, clothing to sell"
- scripture says "she considers land and buys it"
- scripture says "she gives to the poor"

as we can see she wasn't lazy at all! She took care of home and business.

QUESTIONS & ANSWERS

When was the serpent able to deceive Eve?

_____
_____
_____
_____
_____
_____

What plays a vital role in the act of committing sin?

_____
_____
_____
_____
_____
_____

What was the ultimate punishment to Adam & Eve?

_____

_____

_____

_____

_____

_____

How do you feel about the way God dealt with Eve?

_____

_____

_____

_____

_____

_____

Can we change God's order?

_____

_____

_____

_____

_____

_____

CHAPTER THREE

THE BODY

There are very distinctive physical features that make us women. Here's a list of the features:

1. **Breasts- Our breasts are fuller than a man's**
2. **Hair- Our hair generally grows longer than a man's**
3. **Genitalia- We have a vagina and the man a penis**
4. **Pregnancy- Is one of the best privileges we have as women**
5. **Menstruation- Which provides natural cleansing**

In God's creation of the women, He allowed her breasts to be used as a means for providing milk to the infant after childbirth. During pregnancy, the body prepares for lactation which is the process of breastfeeding. What an amazing gift He provided through us women.

Genesis 49:25 says:

"[Even] by the God of thy father, who shall help thee; and by the Almighty, who shall bless thee with blessings of heaven above, blessings of the deep that lieth under, blessings of the breasts, and of the womb:"

When we think of women having hair, we envision her with long hair. The Bible also has something to say about women and hair.

<u>1 Corinthians 11:15 says</u>:

"But if a woman has long hair, it is a glory to her: for [her] hair is given her for a covering."

In the book of Genesis God made it clear He made male and female. Also, after creating man and woman, He gave them a command to *be fruitful and multiply*. Only a man and woman can procreate. One part of being fruitful was given specifically to the woman- she was to carry the child for 9 months and then give birth. The enemy, Satan, tries to confuse the matter but God only gave the privilege of procreating to a man and woman coming together after marriage.

God not only made us beautiful, but he made us all beautifully different. For example, beauty consists of many skin tones, hair types, and body sizes. The diversity of women adds a little spice in our sisterhood. We should never be ashamed of the way God made he's a master builder. So, embrace your true beauty.

In closing, our monthly menstruation helps with the body's natural cleansing process and aids in the preparation for gestation. The menstruation is only mentioned in the Bible once in Isaiah 64:6 in which it was comparing it to our righteousness.

QUESTIONS & ANSWERS

Name one purpose of our breasts?

_____

_____

_____

_____

_____

_____

Does the length of our hair matter to God?

_____

_____

_____

_____

_____

What's the one distinctive role only a woman can do?

_____

_____

_____

_____

_____

_____

(Fill in the blank). Children are a _____ from God. Why?

_____

_____

_____

_____

_____

_____

What is the purpose of menstruation?

_____

_____

_____

_____

_____

_____

EMBRACING GOD'S DESIGN

CHAPTER FOUR

TRUE BEAUTY

We have all heard the saying, *Beauty is in the eye of the beholder* but how many of us believe we are beautiful? Think for a moment to yourself and name all the features, characteristics, and abilities that make you beautiful. In this section, we will discuss what defines beauty biblically.

1. Which is prettier- a red rose or a white rose?

Now how many of you think the red rose is more beautiful versus the white? Why? What is it about the rose of your choice makes you think it is more beautiful than the other? Is it something from your childhood? Or maybe a societal preference?

2. Which is better- short hair or long hair?

How long is your hair? Does it matter to you? Do you judge others differently based on the length of their hair?

These questions above were just some examples to get you thinking about the reality that everyone has their own perception of what's beautiful to them. We are not to judge others based on our own guidelines. The definition of beauty is determined on an individual basis. Now let's read a few scriptures that relate to physical beauty. Please don't forget that the inside should be beautiful as well.

For example: Genesis 49:25, Song of Solomon 7:7, 4:1-4, and Proverbs 31:30 all relate to beauty. There are many more verses that refer to beauty as well. What God finds beautiful and what we typically find beautiful often differs. We should appreciate the distinctive features God gave each one of us. Let's look at this verse:

John 1:3 says:

"All things were made by Him; and without Him was not anything made that was made."

We see in this verse that God created every living thing upon this earth, so we should feel blessed to have such a wonderful Creator who designed each of us.

When God describes us, he says '*We are fearfully and wonderfully made.*' Now that's a powerful declaration! If the God of the universe can say that about you then *we* should value how we were created.

Comparing ourselves to one another only distorts our view of beauty. You were made with distinct features that make you unique. So many women have surgery to alter the way they look. It subconsciously says we feel God made a mistake when He created us. God does everything perfectly and makes no mistakes.

There is one way I learned to accept hoe God made me was appreciating things that made me different. When we choose to focus on the positive things about ourselves it helps sharpens our confidence.

So, the next time you question how beautiful you are, remember that God is a perfectionist and He can do no wrong.

QUESTIONS & ANSWER

Am I beautiful?

_____

_____

_____

_____

_____

_____

Can you name something about yourself that's unique?

_____

_____

_____

_____

_____

_____

(Fill in the blank). Every person God created is
_____.

_____

_____

_____

_____

_____

_____

Does it matter what others think about your physical appearance?

_____

_____

_____

_____

_____

_____

Do you think material things define a woman's beauty?
e.g. (jewelry, clothes, hair, makeup)

_____

_____

_____

_____

_____

_____

CHAPTER FIVE

GIFTS & TALENTS

In this section I would like to start by defining the words <u>gift</u> and <u>talent</u>. The following are the terms:

Gift- something given; a donation; a present

Talent- an inborn ability or aptitude

We see after reading the definitions that a gift is something we receive externally, and a talent is something received internally. Now let's look at examples in the Bible that represent both categories:

DANIEL= who was born with the **talent** of dreams/visions and their interpretations and was also given the **gift** of prophecy by God.

SAMSON=who was born with the **talent** of great strength.

Sorry ladies, I know the examples are men only, but they are great ones! Now let's look at the purpose of having these in our possession. First, the #1 purpose is to bring glory to God. Whenever we're sharing our God given gifts and talents with others, it leads them to Christ. Secondly, our gifts and talents bless others when we do as God commands us. There's no greater reward than giving and sharing. The Bible tells us:

<u>Acts 20:35 says:</u>

"I have shewed you all things, how that so laboring ye ought to support the weak, and to remember the words of the Lord Jesus, how He said, it is more blessed to give than to receive."

Another amazing biblical fact is God doesn't give gifts based on whether you repented or not. Let's read this verse:

Romans 11:29 says:

"For the gifts and calling of God are without repentance."

God is the one who gives, and they're not based on any merit of ourselves as we see in the above scripture. If you want an idea of what your gifts might be, think these things:

- What you have a passion for
- What your good at

After you've done that pray and ask God for direction, our greatest fulfill in life is doing God's will for us. Once you know what your gifts are you can then bless others while bringing glory to God.

If you are struggling to determine your gifts and talents, prayer is a vital component. We should seek God for understanding of our gifts and how they should be used. In closing, be sure to submit every gift and talent under the authority of God, if not then Satan will try to corrupt your gifts for his use.

An example of this would be those who have the gift of a beautiful voice to sing but only produce songs about lust, fornication, and adultery. These individuals allowed Satan to come in and corrupt their gifts. So, remember our abilities will bring glory to God.

QUESTIONS & ANSWERS

What are my gifts?

_____

_____

_____

_____

_____

_____

What are my talents?

_____

_____

_____

_____

_____

_____

How can they bring glory to God?

_____

_____

_____

_____

_____

_____

Can others benefit from my gifts & talents?

_____

_____

_____

_____

_____

_____

Am I sitting down on what God has given me?

_____

_____

_____

_____

_____

_____

CHAPTER SIX

IDENTITY UNLOCKED

In a society where we are constantly asked to verify our identities, some of us get lost in the shuffle. When applying for a loan, house, car or even a credit card there are 2 top identifiers that companies use frequently

1. **Picture I.D.- which identifies you visually**
2. **Social Security Card- which identifies that the name belongs to you**

You may get aggravated after going through this process of identification everywhere you go, but it's for your benefit. Now view this from spiritual of point of view. God knows who belongs to Him as we should know who our God is. Look at these verses:

John 10:27-28 says:

"My sheep hear My voice, and I know them, and they follow Me: And I give unto them eternal life; and they shall never perish, neither shall any man pluck them out of My hand."

John 10:29 says:

"My Father, which gave them Me, is greater than all; and no man is able to pluck them out of My Father's hand:"

Matthew 10:30 says:

"But the very hairs of your head are all numbered:"

Okay if you had any doubt that God knows exactly who you are, it stops here. We must dig a little deeper now, ask yourself this 'Who am I?' Sounds simple yet so complicated for some to know who they are. What makes up our identity? There are common things such as your standards and/or principles, the name you were given, and the area you grew up in that make us who we are or who we will become.

Many of us go through life treating it like an experiment, trying to figure out its meaning. In doing that, we end up wasting time on meaningless things.

To learn more about who you are, you will probably have to refer to the owner's manual, *the Bible*, as your guide. Also, the environments you were exposed to can affect what you allow to mold your identity. To unlock who you are, facing the not-so-good about yourself is necessary.

Learn to talk to God and others by being completely transparent. The journey of discovering who you are can be challenging. You may want to peel back the many layers of learned traits. In my discovery process I started getting rid of traditions and likes/dislikes that were influenced by others. Once I did all that God was able to build me up again.

QUESTIONS & ANSWERS

Who are you?

_____

_____

_____

_____

_____

_____

What are your likes and dislikes?

_____

_____

_____

_____

_____

_____

Do you know your purpose?

_____
_____
_____
_____
_____
_____
_____

What is "fitting in"?

_____
_____
_____
_____
_____
_____

Does your life represent who you are in Christ?

_____

_____

_____

_____

_____

_____

WHO AM I? KNOWING YOUR WORTH

CHAPTER SEVEN

CHOOSING A CAREER

In life as women, we have a lot of things to juggle such as home, children, husband, church, etc. It's very important we learn good time management. All these things directly affect our career choices. As for myself– after years of working, being a stay at home mom, and going to college– I soon realized that a job with flexibility would be the perfect fit for my family.

After completing the Nursing program at the local college, I began looking for jobs with flexible schedules. I want to share what I've learned on this journey of being a working mom. Here a list of questions I asked myself when choosing a job maybe these will help you as well:

Can I work around my responsibilities?

We have many responsibilities along with having others who rely on us. Being able to work and it does not compromise your role as a wife, mother, and your relationship with God is the key.

How about you?

_____

_____

_____

_____

_____

_____

Can it help others in a positive way?

I always thought ministry is serving others. So, I went to college for Nursing because I love helping others and was fascinated with the body related to health. For my readers, you to need find out what you're passionate about and how that could benefit others.

What about *your* job?

_____

_____

_____

_____

_____

_____

What is the stress level?

Now we all know as women, we can get pretty worked up when it's too much going on in our lives. By knowing our tolerance levels, we should aim for a job that wouldn't add more stress or responsibility than we can handle.

What is *your* stress level?

_____

_____

_____

_____

_____

_____

If you look at Proverbs 31:10-31, these verses talk about the virtuous woman. The attributes described in the referenced verses give us a picture of a well-defined businesswoman with integrity. She could manage business, home, and please her husband. I'm not saying it's easy to juggle all those things but with the proper time management, you can.

I want to list just a few things this virtuous woman could accomplish:

1. She worked with her hands (sewing, cooking)

2. She bought land to plant a vineyard

3. She helped the poor and needy

Although she was married with children, she didn't neglect their needs while maintaining a career. I know as a mother it can feel quite overwhelming some days, however, the best asset we have is taking all our cares to God.

When we spend private time with God daily, it makes our load easier to bear. We have a special role to fulfill in our homes and to those in the world. I pray that you find peace in living your purpose per God's design.

I want to share some career paths that can offer flexibility in your role as a mother or wife:

- Billing/Coding
- Nursing
- Home Daycare
- Non-Medical Homecare

When choosing a career, it's not always about the money, in fact those with children must consider a lot more. If you don't have any children yet it's wise to consider all your options before that time comes.

CHAPTER EIGHT

WAITING TO BE FOUND

We all reach the point when we ask the question 'Where is my husband or wife?' It seems like time is passing us by in the waiting stage. But ask yourself this, what am I doing with all this time? Since time is moving, we should be. There are things you can do to help you prepare to be a spouse.

Of course, most of you think getting married is the finale…but only it's the beginning of a journey you must prepare for. Have you ever heard of anyone going on a camping trip without any food, water, or supplies? It's the same principle in marriage. Preparation is key to make it through the unexpected. Ok, let's discuss some simple tools that can help during the waiting phase:

1. **Learn what to look for in your future mate**
    Many of you have an ideal fantasy of what you want in a spouse, but it's not realistic. When it comes to joining your life with another, you need to know what qualities you value. Also, the Bible gives specific information on the roles of husband and wife. You can never go wrong there.
2. **Study/prepare for your new role**
    Now for this tool, the Bible is the foundation for learning your role. You can also invest in books, seminars, videos, workshops from those who have plenty of wisdom and knowledge to share. Maybe in your local church you might have a singles ministry or women's ministry that help young women to prepare as a new wife.
3. **Ask God for direction & trust his timing**
    One of the most important steps in this process is consulting God. We should pray and fast because this is a covenant you will make before God. In the Bible, God tells us how

seriously He views making a vow. While I waited, I began to invest in myself by allowing God to work on areas that needed improvement. I also purchased books, watched videos, prayed and fasted to be better. Although we get our strength from God at times, we can still fall weak to temptation. Once your serious you can wait patiently for the husband God has for you.

QUESTIONS & ANSWERS

Have I prepared for my role?

_____

_____

_____

_____

_____

What does the Bible say about my role?

_____

_____

_____

_____

_____

Are you keeping yourself for your husband?

_____

_____

_____

_____

_____

Have you invested in any books, workshops, or materials as learning tools?

_____

_____

_____

_____

_____

_____

Are you ready for marriage?

_____

_____

_____

_____

_____

_____

CHAPTER NINE

THE POTENTIAL MATE

Okay ladies, what does a godly man look like? Many of you may have asked yourselves a time or two. I want you to imagine for a minute your idea of a godly man. Now, don't use what you've seen in movies or on television because those are unrealistic viewpoints. Usually most of women will tend to look at the men that have been influential in our lives and base our ideas from that.

Secondly, some of your ideas may be tainted from past relationships that were ungodly and not good examples at all. Our main authoritative description of a godly man should always be learned from the Bible. The Bible gives us key attributes to look for which are must haves for the godly man:

1. **He must love God**
2. **He must understand his role as the priest of the home**
3. **He must love his wife as Christ loves the church**
4. **He must be a provider for his family**

Now I know some of us will meet guys who may have one or two of the above qualities, but does it really make sense to compromise? Ask yourself this, let's say he has qualities #2 and #4, right? But how would you feel about the other two that are missing? *He doesn't love God, so he can't love you.*

We can't pick and choose what we will accept. God does everything perfectly so if He gives you a husband, he will be fully equipped in his role. Seek God for guidance in all decisions you make. The joining of two lives can affect your now and your future.

I want to elaborate on certain qualities to look for in a potential mate. A good starting point would be Ephesians chapter 5, gives a few descriptive characteristics. After reading to the scriptures we should examine our experience from past relationships. Ask yourself these questions when analyzing past relationships

- Why didn't it work?
- Did I ignore red flags?
- Are they a man of God?

Doing this will give a better idea of what to look for and what not to accept.

QUESTIONS & ANSWERS

Does he have the Biblical characteristics?

_____

_____

_____

_____

_____

_____

Does he want me to change who I am?

_____

_____

_____

_____

_____

_____

Can he accept God's purpose for my life?

_____

_____

_____

_____

_____

_____

Does he accept my children?

_____

_____

_____

_____

_____

_____

Have I fasted and prayed about him?

_____

_____

_____

_____

_____

_____

WELCOME TO MARRIAGE

CHAPTER TEN

THE VOW

In this chapter, I want to explain the significance of making a vow to God and what it means. Some of us take this lightly as if it has no bearing on our lives. When you make a vow, you are held accountable for keeping it. After intense study, I learned that inner vows are just as important. Have you ever said to yourself, *'I'm not going to do that again,'* and you end up doing it again? Well that's an example of an inner vow. A vow that God has also heard. We should only make vows that we fully understand and desire to keep wholeheartedly.

Let's start this section with the Webster's dictionary meaning of "vow", and the Bible's definition of "vow".

Webster- a solemn promise or assertion; *specifically*: one by which a person is bound to an act, service, or condition

Bible (KJV)- *To give, consecrate or dedicate to God by a solemn promise*

If you read closely, the definitions are very similar. Have you ever paid attention at a wedding when the couple exchanged vows? Do you remember the part when they name all the things that could go wrong or right and that they vow to remain together? Those are vows that we are held accountable for to God and to each other.

If you know your Bible, then you would know that Jesus's first miracle was performed at a wedding. How significant is that! A wedding is a celebration of two people becoming one. There's no greater joy than knowing your husband is the one God ordained just for you. Most of us when taking the wedding vow don't fully understand it. It's not until we are already in it, we then realize what we've done. The Bible tells us that takes a vow very serious, so we should only make when we're sure.

What should you ask yourself before making a vow? The following questions are designed to make you think more in depth about how serious a vow is:

Can I keep this vow?

_____

_____

_____

_____

_____

_____

Can I handle the bad times? Write down something that you've experienced in your life or watched others go through that was bad or rough.

_____

_____

_____

_____

_____

_____

How do you handle it when things go wrong?

_____
_____
_____
_____
_____
_____

What will I have to give up for my spouse?

_____
_____
_____
_____
_____
_____

What does my spouse expect from me?

_____

_____

_____

_____

_____

_____

CHAPTER ELEVEN

THE DEPTH OF INTIMACY

Intimacy is one of those areas that can be defined in many ways. One of the first examples we have is the making of Eve in the Bible. God took a rib from Adam and made Eve. When God puts a man and woman together in a covenant the two become one (spiritually). How can you get any closer than being intimately connected with your spouse? There is a level of intimacy between a husband and wife that can only be accomplished through God. In the Bible, it tells us that in:

Matthew 19:5-6 says:

"And said, for this cause shall a man leave father and mother, and shall cleave to his wife: and they twain shall be one flesh?

Wherefore they are no more twain, but one flesh. What therefore God hath joined, let not man put asunder."

Now that's an intimate bond between man and woman. Most people think of intimacy in a sexual context because in the world today sex sells. The reason so many people associate intimacy with sex is because of Satan's tactic to destroy something God created for our enjoyment.

When you are intimate with your spouse it gives you a level of transparency with no other person besides God. There shouldn't be any fear of being completely open with your spouse, and vice-versa.

One of the foundational principles of intimacy is friendship. Many overlook this an attempt to just rush to the altar. But friendship is a very strong building block in a marriage.

The second thing that intimacy requires is transparency. Many of us want to hide the things that hurt us, the disappointments we experienced, or the insecurities about ourselves. When you are open about all of this, it gives you the freedom to be yourself.

When you keep secrets, it places you in bondage and induces fear of being rejected should the truth be made known. Being transparent provides a level of freedom that promotes growth and a healthy mental state. A wise person values intimacy with God and their spouse.

Growing up I always thought of intimacy in a sexual way...boy was I wrong! It's only when I got, I realized that true intimacy is being vulnerable with your spouse. Your spouse should be a safe place for you to be completely open. A few examples of strengthen this bond would be:

- Reading/studying the Bible together
- Praying for each other
- Talking about your concerns

Remember honesty is the best foundation.

QUESTIONS & ANSWERS

Can you name three godly marriages in the Bible?

_____

_____

_____

_____

_____

Are you ready to share everything with your spouse?

_____

_____

_____

_____

_____

What have you been taught about intimacy?

_____
_____
_____
_____
_____
_____
_____

Do you have an intimate relationship with God?

_____
_____
_____
_____
_____
_____

What are your fears in marriage?

_____

_____

_____

_____

_____

_____

CHAPTER TWELVE

WELCOME TO MOTHERHOOD

In this section I want to list what the Bible says about mothers:

Psalm 127:3 says:

"Lo, children [are] a heritage of the LORD: [and] the fruit of the womb [is his] reward."

Psalm 113:9 says:

"He maketh the barren woman to keep house, [and to be] a joyful mother of children. Praise ye the LORD."

Proverbs 1:8 says:

"My son, hear the instruction of thy father, and forsake not the law of thy mother":

Isaiah 49:1 says:

"Listen, O isles, unto me; and hearken, ye people, from far; The LORD hath called me from the womb; from the bowels of my mother hath he made mention of my name".

Ezekiel 19:10 says:

"Thy mother [is] like a vine in thy blood, planted by the waters: she was fruitful and full of branches by reason of many waters".

These are all but a few examples on what the Bible says about mothers. Our roles as mothers are very important to God. We have the opportunity of spending more time with our children than they will with their father. It is our responsibility to be godly examples to our children because they are watching us.

As a mother, we are to teach our children manners, respect of others, cleanliness, and to honor God. If you weren't taught certain principles, that is not an excuse not to teach your children. We must remember children are God's heritage that He's entrusting you as a mother to be responsible for.

The role of the mother is a very important position. We are the main caregiver, who the one who help shape our children lives. When molding their characters, we should find ways to input the Bible in ways they can understand.

The most important part is being married to your God ordained husband who will provide your children with a godly foundation and stability. I know it's easy to think our roles are overlooked and not appreciated as we would like, but the God of the universe notices.

I love the fact that Jesus was on the cross about to take His last breath but wanted to make sure that His mother Mary would be cared for after His death. Now how many of you would think about that before taking your last breath? This tells me that Jesus valued His mother and her role in His life. I suggest you go read this in John 19:26-27 as it gives understanding of how important it is being a mother.

In recent years Homeschooling has become a great alternative to public school. More mothers are making this selection to have time to teach their children core values. If you need in any area of motherhood and making the best decisions for your children, ask God. Remember to start everyday will prayer and asking for God's strength.

QUESTIONS & ANSWERS

Can you list godly characteristics of a mother?

_____

_____

_____

_____

_____

_____

Can you list ungodly characteristics of a mother?

_____

_____

_____

_____

_____

_____

Is there anything you want to change before you become a mother?

_____

_____

_____

_____

_____

_____

Do you have any fears about having children?

_____

_____

_____

_____

_____

_____

Are you ready to take on the responsibility?

_____

_____

_____

_____

_____

_____

ABOUT KINSHAWDA DANIELS

Kinshawda Daniels is a devoted mother, a driven businesswoman, and the Founder of "OFF THE HAMSTER WHEEL INC with a passion in health and wellness. She gives a lot of her time to women empowerment with a focus on young girls. Her dream is to impact the lives of women all over the world.

As a Certified Life Coach, she offers compassionate coaching to those that desire to break negative cycles in their lives. She's always had a love for health hence the reason she became a nurse. As a Licensed Practical Nurse helping women make healthier choices is something, she's passionate about. Kinshawda realizes that spiritual health and physical health should be treated equal.

SPECIAL THANKS

I would like to thank the many supporters of my vision and for believing in me. I'm thankful to all my family and friends who not only supported me but invested your time, money, and love into this book.

CONTACT INFORMATION

INSTAGRAM   @kinshawda

FACEBOOK   @kinshawdadaniels

TWITTER   @kinshawda

PERISCOPE   @kinshawdadaniels

YOUTUBE   @Kinshawda Daniels

Made in the USA
Columbia, SC
08 April 2022